Skyways

Knights and Castles

Anne Rowe

Life in a Castle

By about 1200 AD a castle was a big square building called a *keep*. This had a strong stone wall all round it and perhaps a wide ditch filled with water called a *moat*.

The square keep at Hedingham Castle, 1140.

A rich lord and his family lived in a castle. Knights lived in the castle too.

The great hall was the most important room in the castle. This is where people ate and were entertained. There was very little furniture, just large tables with chairs for the lord, his family, the knights and servants.

The great hall at Conwy Castle in Wales as it might have appeared at the end of the 13th century.

Most people slept on the floor. The lord and lady had a bed, with a feather mattress and pillows. There were curtains all round it to keep out the draughts. They did not wear night clothes, but they did have nightcaps.

A castle had a number of toilets, called *garderobes*. Some were just a ledge stuck out over the moat. Others were built at the top of the walls over a long shaft that went to a cesspit. The seat was just a slab of stone with a round hole cut in it.

A Day in a Castle

The day began at sunrise. After church, everyone went to work. The peasants would work on the land outside the castle walls. Work stopped at 10 o'clock when the trumpet or bell sounded for dinner time.

Ploughing in medieval times.

They ate dinner in the great hall. Everyone sat in their own place. It showed how important they were in the castle.

Wooden bowls were put on the table. There was a piece of bread in the bowl to mop up the gravy. They ate a lot of stews and drank wine or ale.

A medieval banquet.

After dinner the lord of the castle might go hunting.

A lord and his family out hunting with their hawks.

The women might sew until suppertime.

After sunset there would be some entertainment at the castle. Perhaps jugglers or a storyteller would visit the castle and entertain the crowd.

Defending a Castle

When a lord was going to build a castle which would be hard to attack, he looked for a good spot to build on, like on top of a hill. It was hard for the attackers to fight uphill.

The walls of a castle were very thick, often as much as seven metres wide. The outer walls had towers built into them so that if the castle was under attack all parts of the wall could be seen from inside the castle.

Harlech Castle in Wales was built in the late 13th century on top of a hill. It has large round towers at each corner.

The top of the outer wall had its own defences. The walls had *crenellations* along the top. This allowed archers to hide behind the stone defences after firing their bows and arrows in the gaps.

The enemy soldiers usually attacked the gate of the castle first. Castle builders, therefore, made the gate very strong. A *portcullis* and a *drawbridge* would be added to it.

When under attack the drawbridge across the moat would be pulled up and the portcullis brought down.

The portcullis at Carlisle Castle.

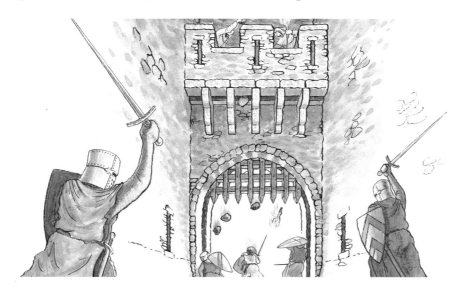

Holes were made in the roof of the gateway entrance. If attackers were able to get inside, the soldiers in the castle would drop stones through the "murder holes". Boiling liquids and flaming torches could also be thrown down.

Even if the enemy soldiers broke through the outer wall, they found it very hard to get into the keep. The lord made sure that there was always a year's supply of food in the cellars. A good castle would have a well inside the keep. If the enemy surrounded the castle, laying *siege* to it, those inside would have enough to eat and drink.

Attacking a Castle

A medieval castle under attack.

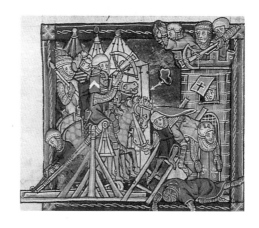

There were different ways of attacking a castle.

1) The enemy tried to get over the castle walls by using *scaling ladders* and *siege towers*. Siege towers were big wooden platforms on wheels which could be moved right up to the castle walls.

2) The enemy tried to knock in the castle walls by using *battering rams*. *Catapults* were also used and were very powerful and could hurl nearly 300 kilogrammes of rocks at a castle wall.

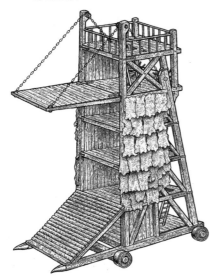

Siege tower.

Catapult.

3) The enemy soldiers tried to get under the wall of the castle by mining. Mining the walls of a castle took a long time.

The *sappers*, or diggers, dug a tunnel under the moat and under the walls. They were protected from the archers in the castle by a wooden shed built above them. The sappers put in timber props to keep up the roof of the tunnel.

When the tunnel was long enough, it was filled with branches and twigs and set on fire. This brought the tunnel down, and with it the castle walls too.

Those inside the castle listened for any sound of miners at work.

Becoming a Knight

Not everyone could train to be a knight. It took a long
time, up to seven years. The training began when a boy
became a *squire* to a knight. A squire was a servant and
it was a hard life. The knight trained the squire.
There was a great ceremony when the squire was made a
knight.

First the squire had to have
a bath. He was dressed in
clean, white clothes with a
long, red robe on top.

He had to spend the whole night in church praying.
This was called the *vigil*. All of his new armour was
laid out on the altar. At dawn everyone came to a
special service.

The young man was presented to his lord by the knight who had trained him. His new armour was put on. The lord himself put on the spurs. The lord touched the young man on each shoulder with a sword.

The young man took the oath of the knight. Then suddenly he was hit very hard. This was said to be the only blow a knight was to take without hitting back.

After all of this, there was a great feast.

The Tournament

Knights fought in real battles but they also fought in mock battles called *tournaments*. These could be very dangerous and some knights were killed.

The ground where the tournaments were held was called the *list*. The knight arrived at the ground two or three days before the fights to rest his horse and to get ready. The squire did most of the work.

Two knights jousting.

The knight had to display his banner during the tournament. The tournaments lasted for four days. There were fights, called *jousts*, each day and feasts every night.

There were prizes for the winning knights and they could become very rich if they were good with a sword or a lance.

Knights displaying their banners during a tournament.

A Knight's Weapons

A knight carried a sword. It was his most important weapon. Some knights used a lance but these often broke when they made a good hit so that the knight needed a second weapon. The battle–axe was very heavy. The mace was used in hand-to-hand fighting.

The knight was protected by wearing heavy metal *armour.*

A model in the Tower of London of a knight in armour on his horse.

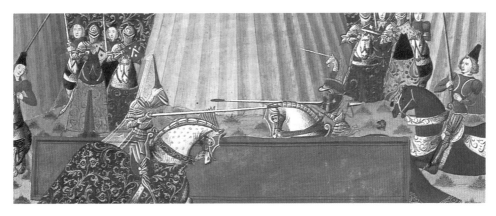

Knights jousting at a tournament with lances.

Clothes in the 13th Century

Castles were often very cold and damp although there were fireplaces in the great hall and the lord's bedroom. Everyone had to wear warm clothes. Most people wore hats, even indoors.

The very rich wore robes of silk and velvet and the poor wore coarse wool. Buttons had just come in, in 1200 AD, but at that time no one had invented the pocket. Fashions did change but very slowly.

Children did not have any special clothes. They wore small copies of grown-up's clothing.

A nobleman and his family.

Clothes in the middle ages told people a lot about the wearer. There were many laws which said what the different classes of people could wear.

The length of the robe was important. A nobleman could wear his robe to the ankles, a richman's robe could go down to his calf but a poor man's tunic could only go as far as his knees.

A merchant.   *A peasant.*

Glossary

Armour A covering made of metal or chain mail which protected the wearer from injury in battle.

Crenellations The stone 'teeth' on top of a castle wall or tower.

Joust A fight between two knights on horseback using lances and other weapons. The jousts took place at Tournaments.

Keep A tall square building inside a strong wall where the lord of the castle and his family lived. At first they were made of wood and later stone. Shell keeps were round instead of square.

Lance A long weapon with a pointed head used by knights on horseback.

Mace A short rod with a spiked metal head on the end which was used as a weapon in the middle ages.

Mining To dig a tunnel under the walls of a castle to cause the collapse of the walls.

Moat A wide ditch round the walls of a castle. It was dug and filled with water to protect the castle from attack.

Portcullis An iron, or sometimes wooden, grating guarding the entrance to a castle.

Siege To lay siege to a castle means to completely surround the castle and to cut off everything going in or out of the castle.

Spurs A sharp spiked wheel fixed to the heel of a knight's shoe which he wore when riding his horse.